THE ESSENTIAL HYMN ANTHOLOGY

- PIANO LEVEL -
INTERMEDIATE TO ADVANCED

ISBN 978-1-70513-484-9

HAL•LEONARD®

For all works contained herein:
Unauthorized copying, arranging, adapting, recording, internet posting, public performance,
or other distribution of the music in this publication is an infringement of copyright.
Infringers are liable under the law.

Visit Hal Leonard Online at
www.halleonard.com

Visit Phillip at
www.phillipkeveren.com

Contact us:
Hal Leonard
7777 West Bluemound Road
Milwaukee, WI 53213
Email: info@halleonard.com

In Europe, contact:
Hal Leonard Europe Limited
42 Wigmore Street
Marylebone, London, W1U 2RN
Email: info@halleonardeurope.com

In Australia, contact:
Hal Leonard Australia Pty. Ltd.
4 Lentara Court
Cheltenham, Victoria, 3192 Australia
Email: info@halleonard.com.au

BIOGRAPHY

Phillip Keveren, a multi-talented keyboard artist and composer, has composed original works in a variety of genres from piano solo to symphonic orchestra. He gives frequent concerts and workshops for teachers and their students in the United States, Canada, Europe, and Asia. Mr. Keveren holds a B.M. in composition from California State University Northridge and a M.M. in composition from the University of Southern California.

PREFACE

The arrangements in this anthology were written over a span of 20 years, originally published in nine different folios (detailed on pages 146–147). We chose some of our favorites, then added four new settings to round out the collection. The hymns arranged especially for this book are "Doxology," "Great Is Thy Faithfulness," "Just As I Am," and "We Gather Together."

I love writing hymn arrangements. The tunes are sturdy, inspired, and timeless. The texts are the bedrock of Christian faith. The process of making a hymn sing at the piano is a task of which I never tire.

I hope you find some of your favorites in this book!

Blessings,

Phillip Keveren

CONTENTS

ABIDE WITH ME

Words by HENRY F. LYTE
Music by WILLIAM H. MONK
Arranged by Phillip Keveren

Yearning (♩ = 69–76)

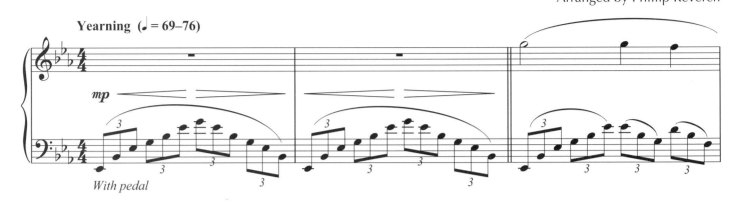

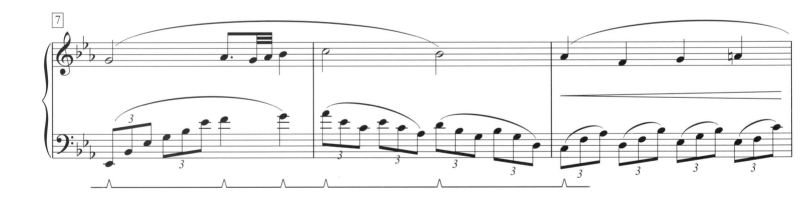

Copyright © 2011 by HAL LEONARD CORPORATION
International Copyright Secured   All Rights Reserved

ALL CREATURES OF
OUR GOD AND KING

Music from *Geistliche Kirchengesang*
Arranged by Phillip Keveren

Copyright © 2018 by HAL LEONARD LLC
International Copyright Secured   All Rights Reserved

AMERICA, THE BEAUTIFUL

Words by KATHERINE LEE BATES
Music by SAMUEL A. WARD
Arranged by Phillip Keveren

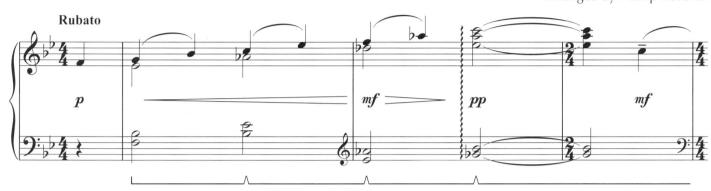

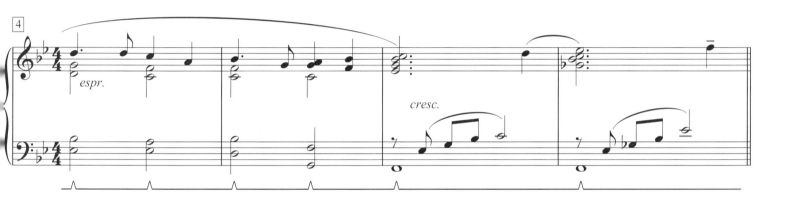

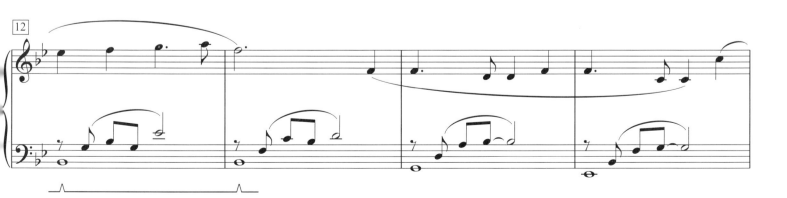

Copyright © 2002 by HAL LEONARD CORPORATION
International Copyright Secured   All Rights Reserved

AMAZING GRACE

Traditional American Melody
Arranged by Phillip Keveren

Copyright © 2018 by HAL LEONARD LLC
International Copyright Secured   All Rights Reserved

AT CALVARY

Words by WILLIAM R. NEWELL
Music by DANIEL B. TOWNER
Arranged by Phillip Keveren

Copyright © 2017 by HAL LEONARD LLC
International Copyright Secured   All Rights Reserved

BE THOU MY VISION

Traditional Irish
Arranged by Phillip Keveren

Copyright © 2011 by HAL LEONARD CORPORATION
International Copyright Secured   All Rights Reserved

BATTLE HYMN OF THE REPUBLIC

Words by JULIA WARD HOWE
Music by WILLIAM STEFFE
Arranged by Phillip Keveren

Slowly, reverently (♩ = 78)

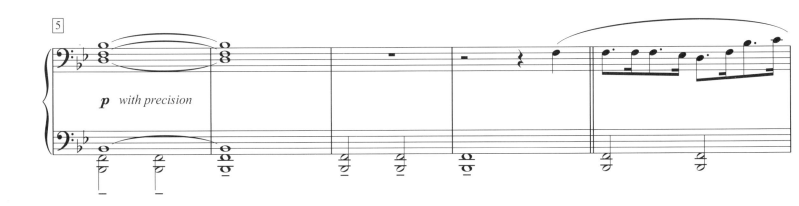

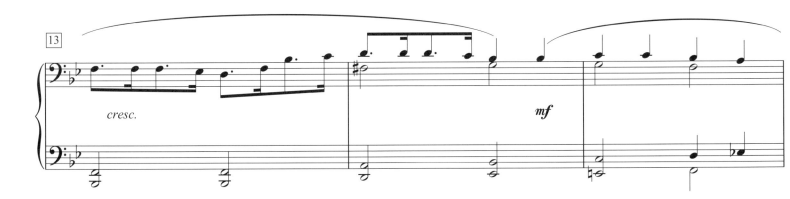

Copyright © 2002 by HAL LEONARD CORPORATION
International Copyright Secured   All Rights Reserved

CHRIST THE LORD IS RISEN TODAY

Words by CHARLES WESLEY
Music adapted from *Lyra Davidica*
Arranged by Phillip Keveren

With fanfare (♩ = 100)

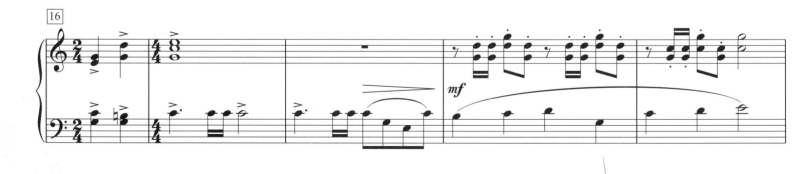

Copyright © 2017 by HAL LEONARD LLC
International Copyright Secured   All Rights Reserved

COME, THOU FOUNT OF EVERY BLESSING

Words by ROBERT ROBINSON
Music by *The Sacred Harp*
Arranged by Phillip Keveren

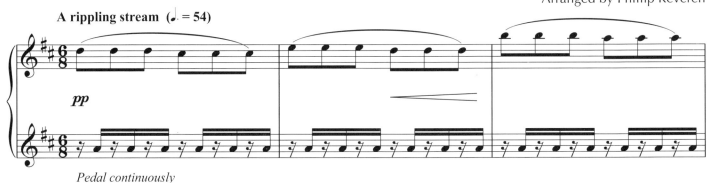

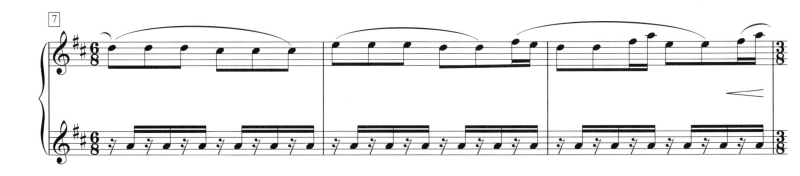

Copyright © 2003 by HAL LEONARD CORPORATION
International Copyright Secured   All Rights Reserved

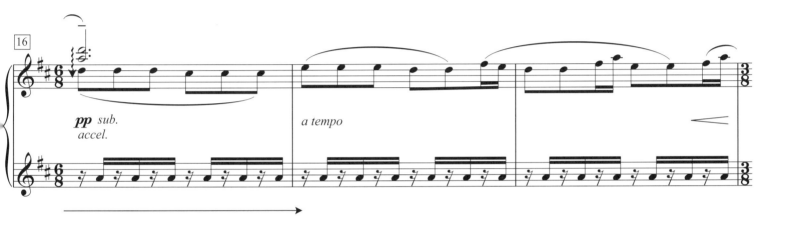

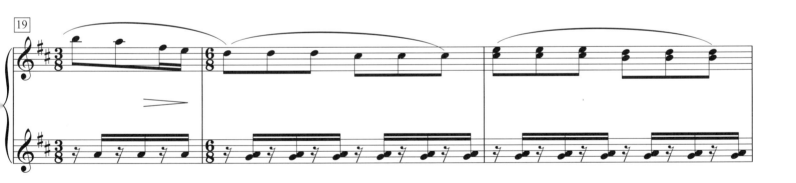

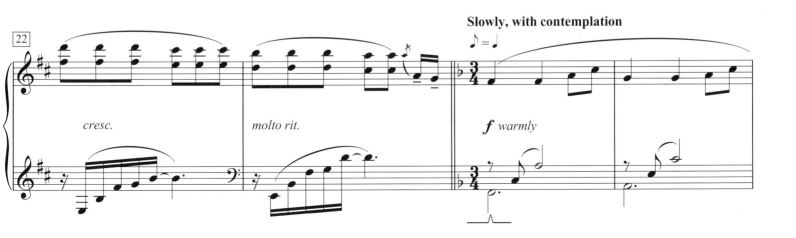

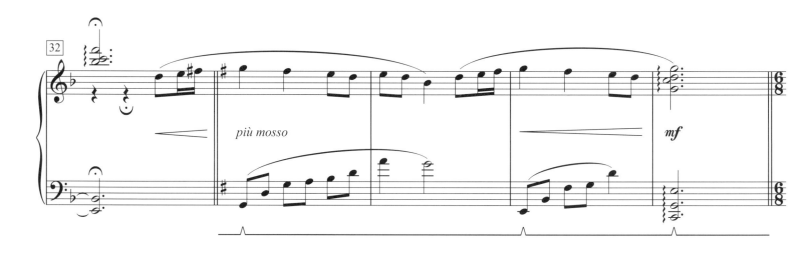

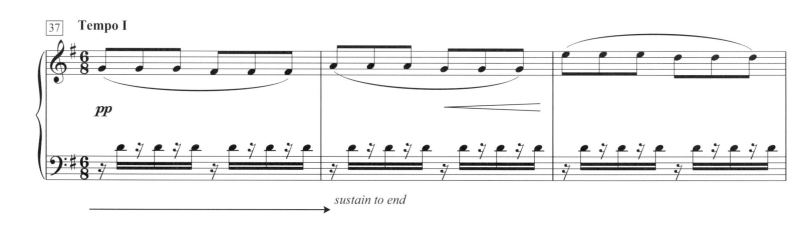

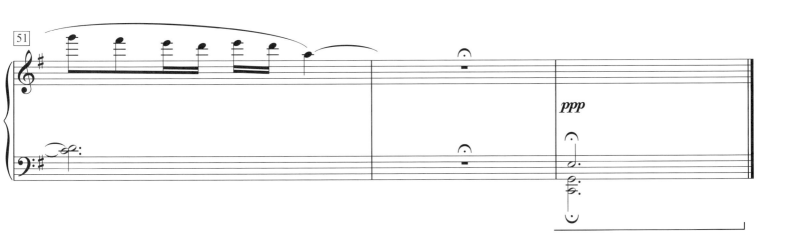

CROWN HIM WITH MANY CROWNS

Words by MATTHEW BRIDGES and GODFREY THRING
Music by GEORGE JOB ELVEY
Arranged by Phillip Keveren

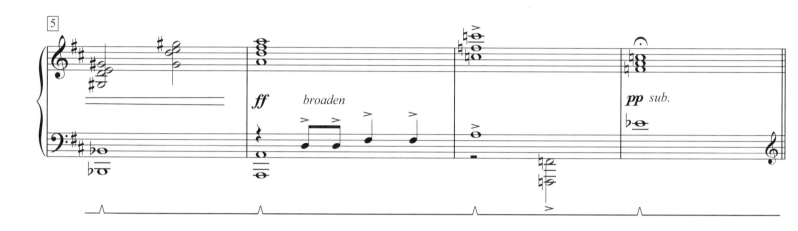

Copyright © 2003 by HAL LEONARD CORPORATION
International Copyright Secured   All Rights Reserved

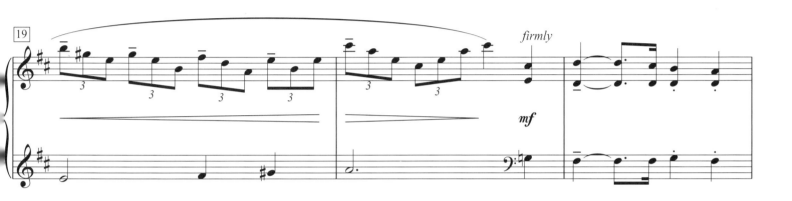

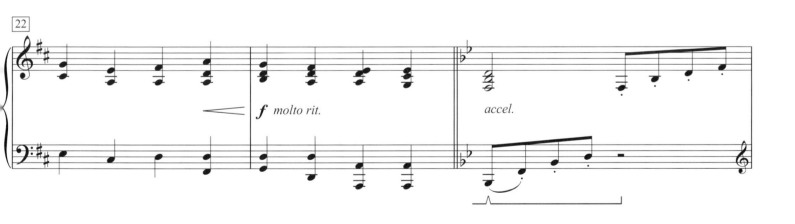

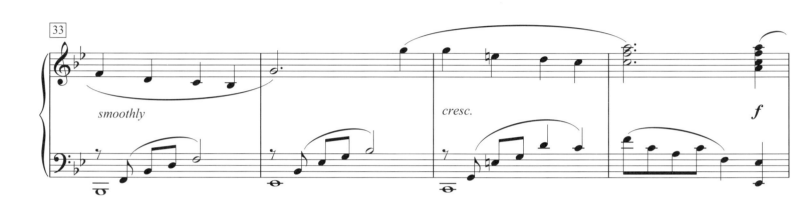

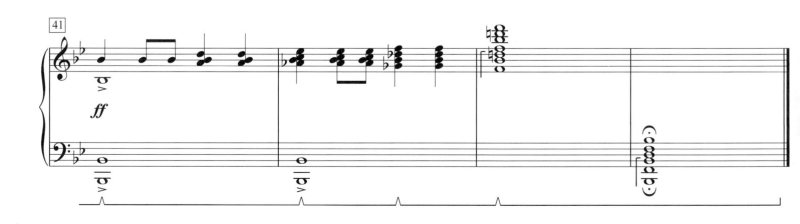

DEEP RIVER

African American Spiritual
Based on Joshua 3
Arranged by Phillip Keveren

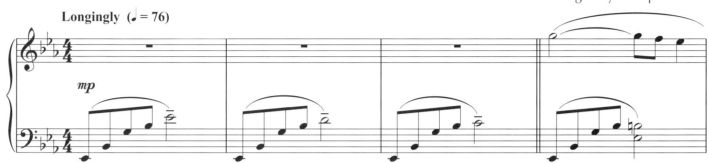

Copyright © 2010 by HAL LEONARD CORPORATION
International Copyright Secured   All Rights Reserved

DOXOLOGY

Traditional
Arranged by Phillip Keveren

Copyright © 2021 by HAL LEONARD LLC
International Copyright Secured   All Rights Reserved

FAITH OF OUR FATHERS

Music by HENRI F. HEMY
and JAMES G. WALTON
Arranged by Phillip Keveren

Expressively, with rubato (♩. = c. 69)

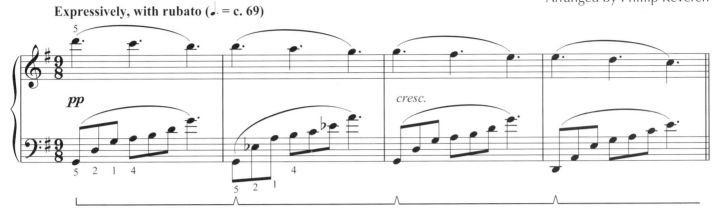

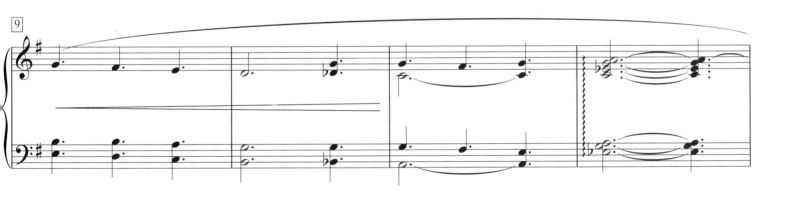

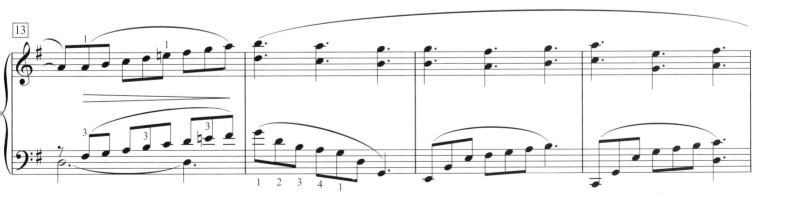

Copyright © 2018 by HAL LEONARD LLC
International Copyright Secured   All Rights Reserved

ETERNAL FATHER, STRONG TO SAVE
(The Navy Hymn)

Words by WILLIAM WHITING
Music by JOHN BACCHUS DYKES
Arranged by Phillip Keveren

Slowly, freely, with conviction

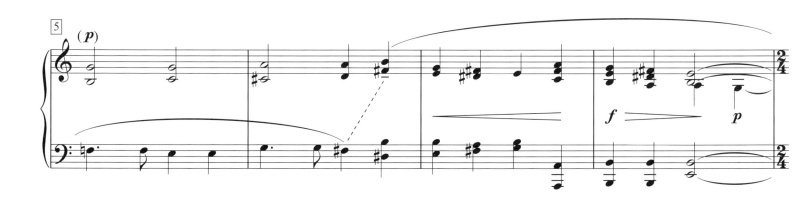

Più mosso

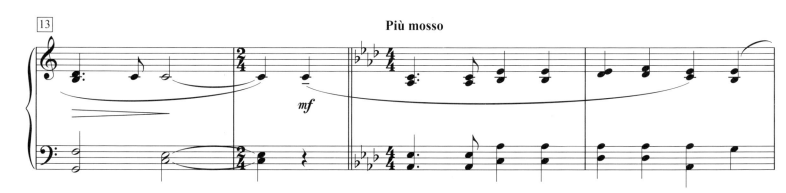

Copyright © 2002 by HAL LEONARD CORPORATION
International Copyright Secured   All Rights Reserved

FAIREST LORD JESUS

Words from *Münster Gesangbuch*
Music from *Schlesische Volkslieder*
Arranged by Phillip Keveren

Slowly, freely

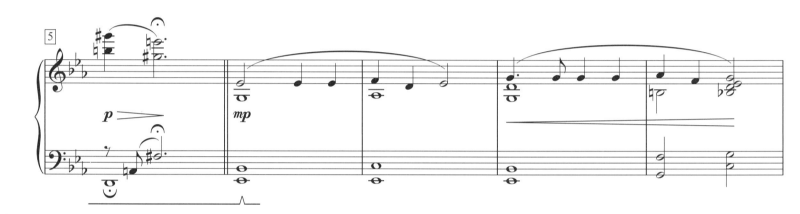

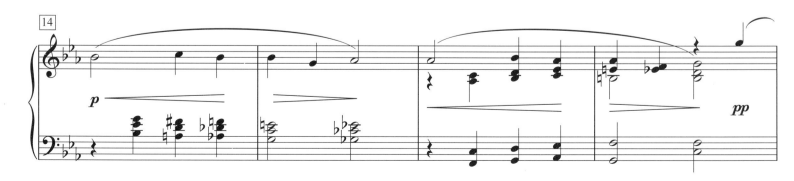

Copyright © 2005 by HAL LEONARD CORPORATION
International Copyright Secured   All Rights Reserved

GOD OF OUR FATHERS

Words by DANIEL CRANE ROBERTS
Music by GEORGE WILLIAM WARREN
Arranged by Phillip Keveren

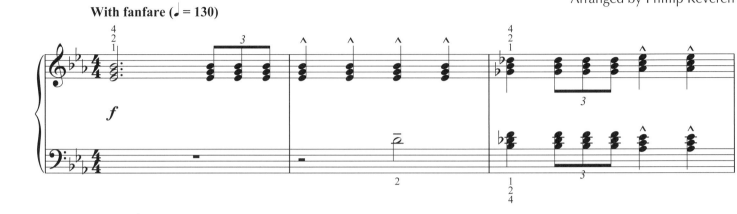

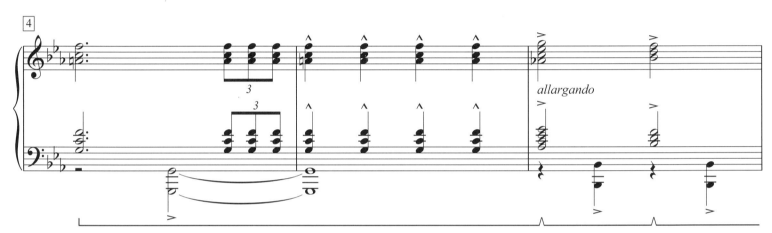

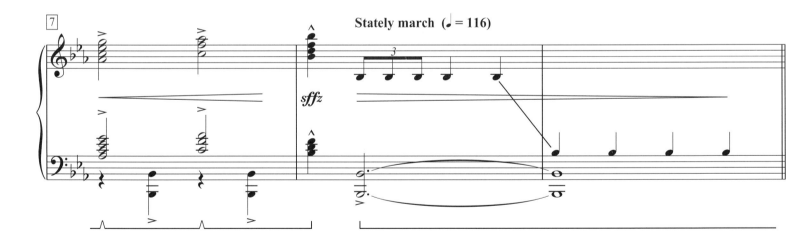

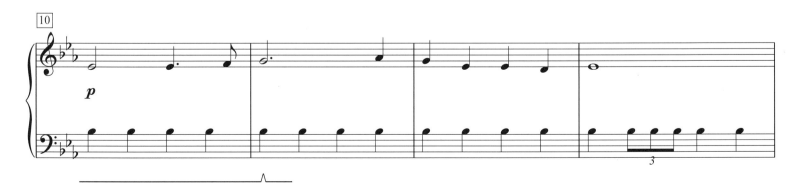

Copyright © 2002 by HAL LEONARD CORPORATION
International Copyright Secured   All Rights Reserved

GREAT IS THY FAITHFULNESS

Words by THOMAS O. CHISHOLM
Music by WILLIAM M. RUNYAN
Arranged by Phillip Keveren

Copyright © 2021 by HAL LEONARD LLC
International Copyright Secured   All Rights Reserved

GUIDE ME, O THOU GREAT JEHOVAH

Words by WILLIAM WILLIAMS
Music by JOHN HUGHES
Arranged by Phillip Keveren

Moderately flowing (♩ = 92)

Copyright © 2011 by HAL LEONARD CORPORATION
International Copyright Secured   All Rights Reserved

HE HIDETH MY SOUL

Inspired by Dvořák's Symphony No. 9 ("From the New World")

Words by FANNY J. CROSBY
Music by WILLIAM J. KIRKPATRICK
Arranged by Phillip Keveren

Copyright © 2017 by HAL LEONARD LLC
International Copyright Secured   All Rights Reserved

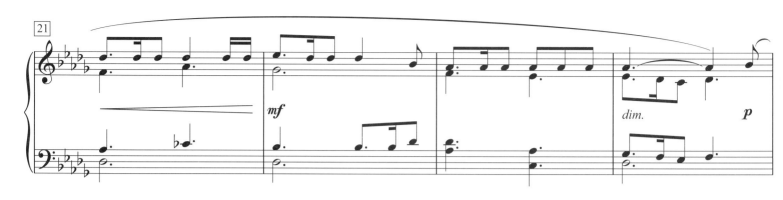

HIS EYE IS ON THE SPARROW

Music by CHARLES H. GABRIEL
Arranged by Phillip Keveren

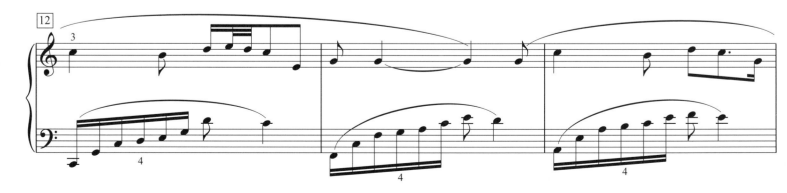

Copyright © 2018 by HAL LEONARD LLC
International Copyright Secured   All Rights Reserved

HYMNS OF THE CROSS

Incorporates "The Old Rugged Cross," "Nothing but the Blood," and "When I Survey the Wondrous Cross"

Arranged by Phillip Keveren

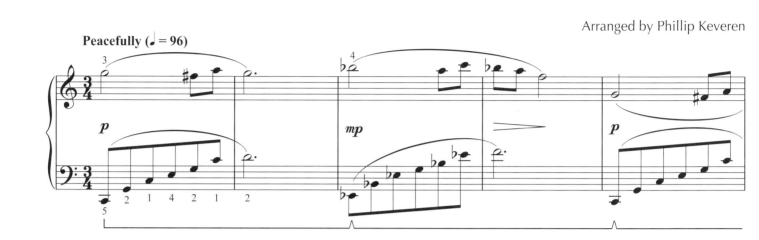

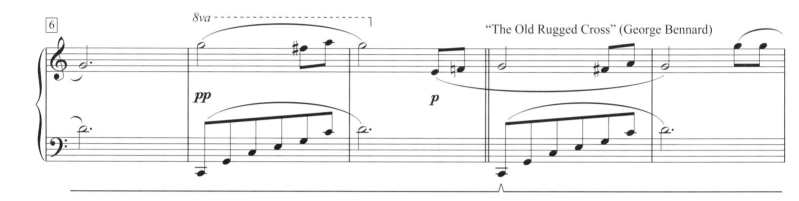

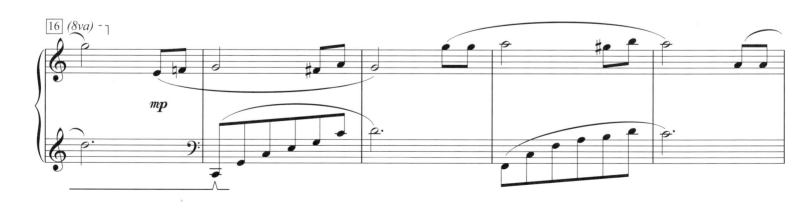

Copyright © 2007 by HAL LEONARD CORPORATION
International Copyright Secured   All Rights Reserved

"Nothing But the Blood" (Robert Lowry)

"When I Survey the Wondrous Cross" (Lowell Mason)

HYMNS OF MAJESTY

Incorporates "A Mighty Fortress Is Our God," "Holy, Holy, Holy! Lord God Almighty," and "Immortal, Invisible"

Arranged by Phillip Keveren

"A Mighty Fortress Is Our God" (Martin Luther)

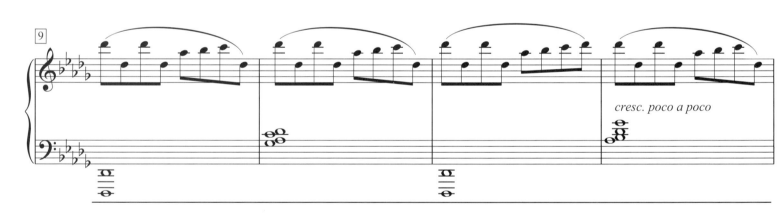

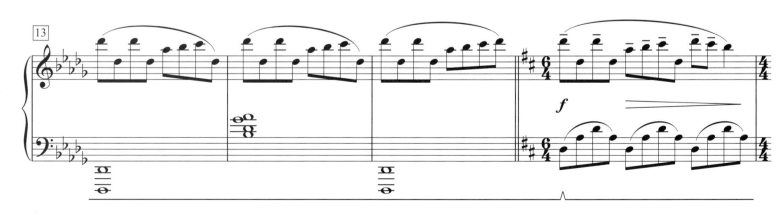

Copyright © 2007 by HAL LEONARD CORPORATION
International Copyright Secured   All Rights Reserved

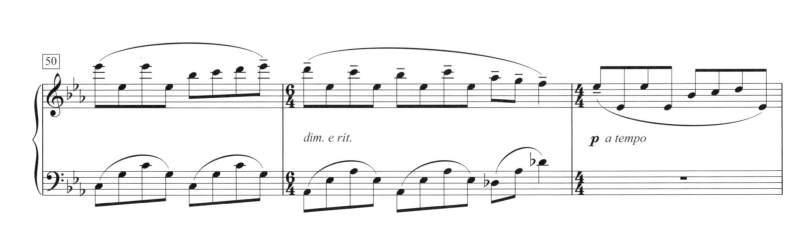

"Holy, Holy, Holy! Lord God Almighty" (John B. Dykes)

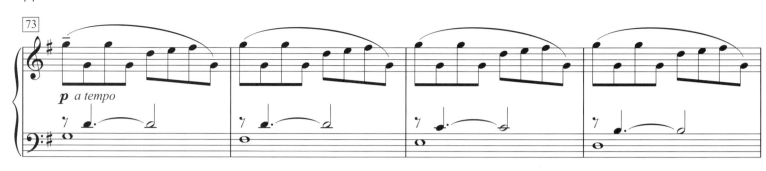

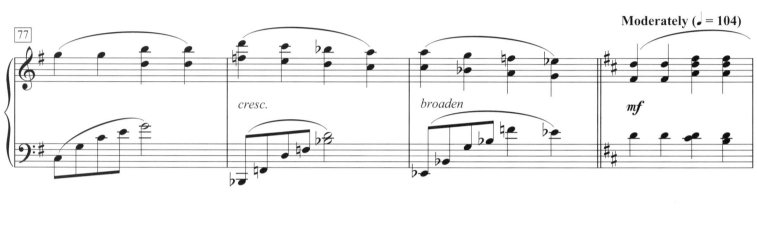

"Immortal, Invisible" (Traditional Welsh Melody)

Stately (♩ = 104)

HYMNS OF PEACE

Incorporates "I've Got Peace Like a River," "Wonderful Peace," and "It Is Well with My Soul"

Arranged by Phillip Keveren

"I've Got Peace Like a River" (Traditional)

Copyright © 2007 by HAL LEONARD CORPORATION
International Copyright Secured   All Rights Reserved

($\flat$ = 104)

"Wonderful Peace" (W.G. Cooper)

"It Is Well with My Soul" (Philip P. Bliss)

I LOVE TO TELL THE STORY

Words by A. CATHERINE HANKEY
Music by WILLIAM G. FISCHER
Arranged by Phillip Keveren

Slowly, lyrically

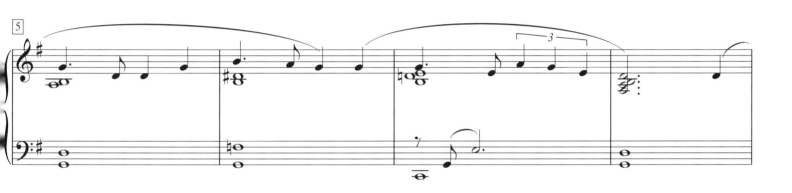

Copyright © 2005 by HAL LEONARD CORPORATION
International Copyright Secured   All Rights Reserved

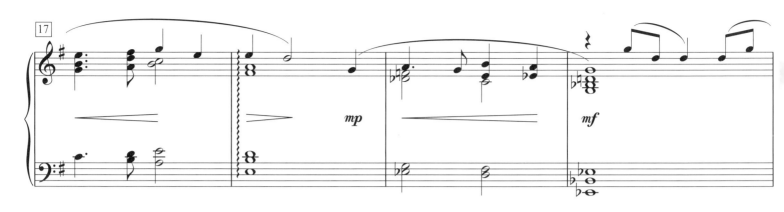

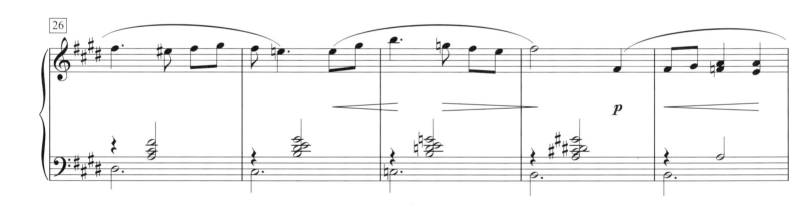

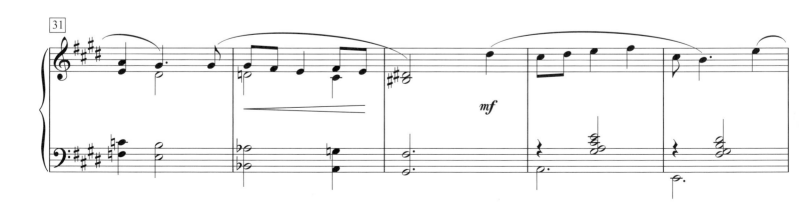

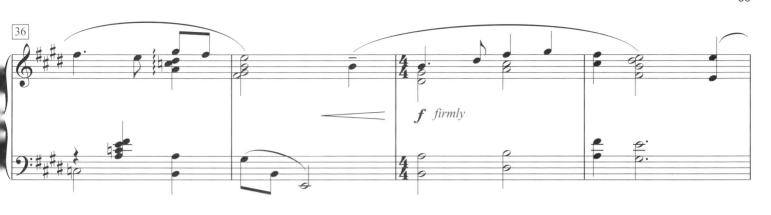

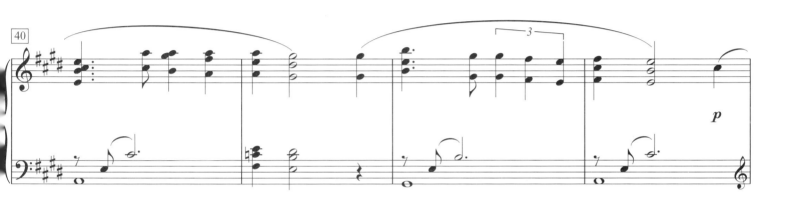

I NEED THEE EVERY HOUR

Inspired by Tchaikovsky's Symphony No. 5 (Third Movement "Waltz")

Words by ANNIE S. HAWKS
Music by ROBERT LOWRY
Arranged by Phillip Keveren

Copyright © 2017 by HAL LEONARD LLC
International Copyright Secured   All Rights Reserved

I SING THE MIGHTY POWER OF GOD

Words by ISAAC WATTS
Music from *Gesangbuch der Herzogl*
Arranged by Phillip Keveren

Copyright © 2018 by HAL LEONARD LLC
International Copyright Secured   All Rights Reserved

IN THE GARDEN

Words and Music by
C. AUSTIN MILES
Arranged by Phillip Keveren

Quietly, with freedom (♩. = 42)

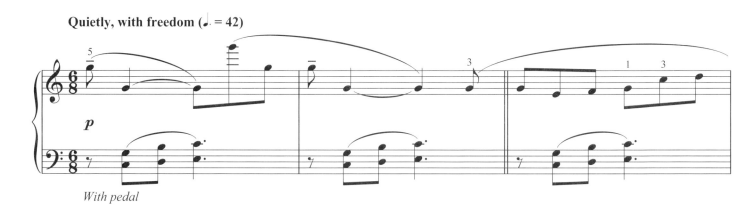

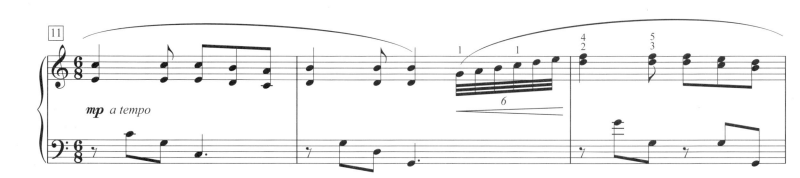

Copyright © 2018 by HAL LEONARD LLC
International Copyright Secured   All Rights Reserved

JESUS IS ALL THE WORLD TO ME

Words and Music by
WILL L. THOMPSON
Arranged by Phillip Keveren

Copyright © 2005 by HAL LEONARD CORPORATION
International Copyright Secured   All Rights Reserved

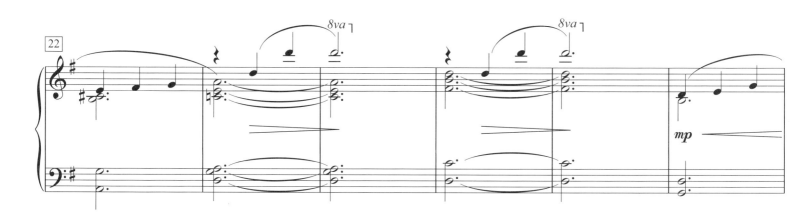

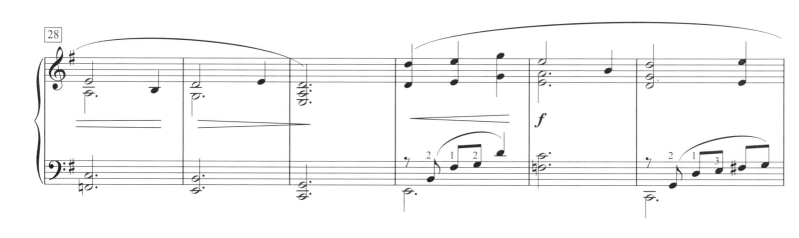

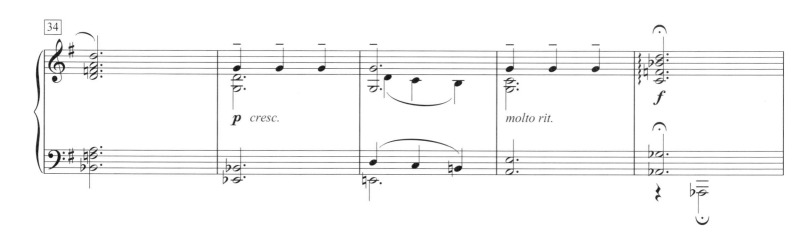

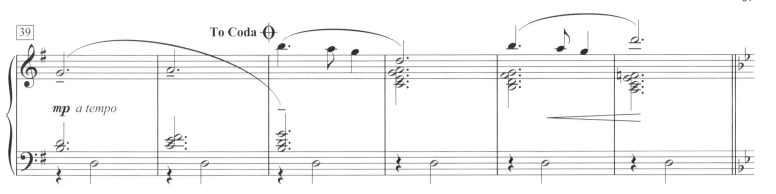

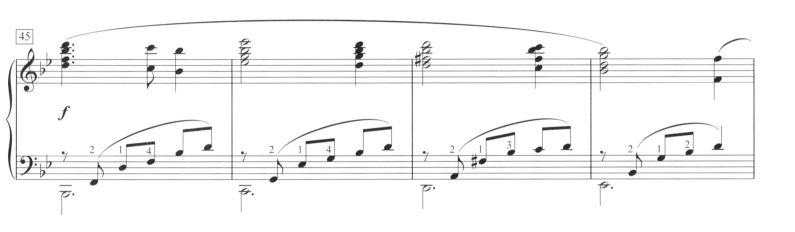

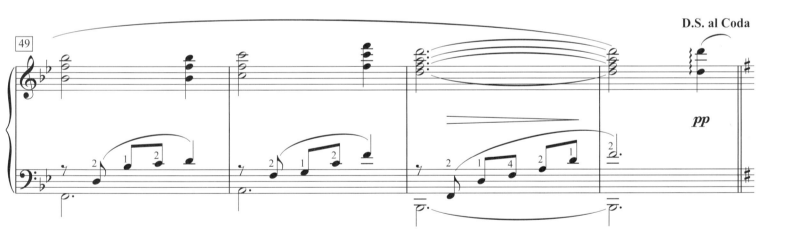

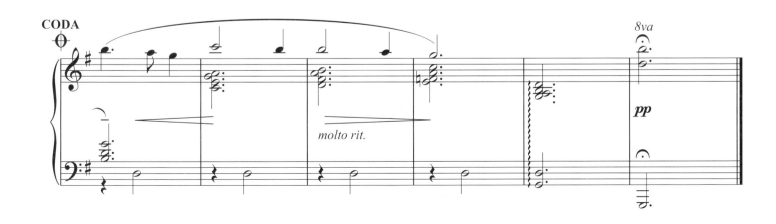

I SURRENDER ALL

Words by J.W. VAN DeVENTER
Music by W.S. WEEDEN
Arranged by Phillip Keveren

Copyright © 2003 by HAL LEONARD CORPORATION
International Copyright Secured   All Rights Reserved

JUST AS I AM
(with Erik Satie's Gymnopédie No. 2)

Words by CHARLOTTE ELLIOTT
Music by WILLIAM B. BRADBURY and ERIK SATIE
Arranged by Phillip Keveren

Copyright © 2021 by HAL LEONARD LLC
International Copyright Secured   All Rights Reserved

LET US BREAK BREAD TOGETHER

Traditional Spiritual
Arranged by Phillip Keveren

Copyright © 2010 by HAL LEONARD CORPORATION
International Copyright Secured   All Rights Reserved

MY COUNTRY, 'TIS OF THEE
(America)

Words by SAMUEL FRANCIS SMITH
Music from *Thesaurus Musicus*
Arranged by Phillip Keveren

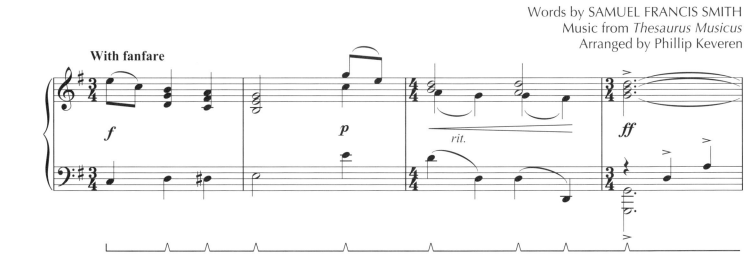

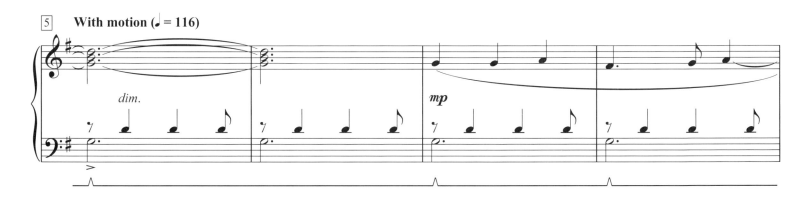

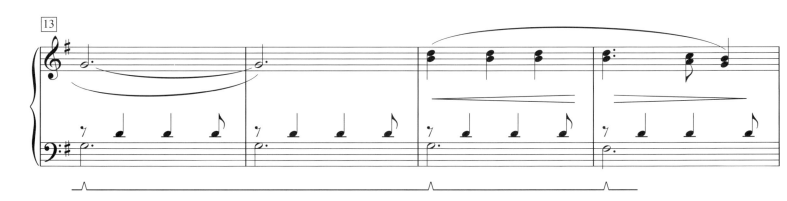

Copyright © 2002 by HAL LEONARD CORPORATION
International Copyright Secured   All Rights Reserved

THE LORD'S MY SHEPHERD, I'LL NOT WANT

Music by JESSIE S. IRVINE
Arranged by Phillip Keveren

Copyright © 2018 by HAL LEONARD LLC
International Copyright Secured   All Rights Reserved

MORNING HAS BROKEN

Traditional Gaelic Melody
Arranged by Phillip Keveren

Copyright © 2018 by HAL LEONARD LLC
International Copyright Secured   All Rights Reserved

O LOVE THAT WILT NOT LET ME GO

Words by GEORGE MATHESON
Music by ALBERT LISTER PEACE
Arranged by Phillip Keveren

Copyright © 2011 by HAL LEONARD CORPORATION
International Copyright Secured   All Rights Reserved

O WORSHIP THE KING

Music attributed to
JOHANN MICHAEL HAYDN
Arranged by Phillip Keveren

In celebration (♩. = 120)

Copyright © 2018 by HAL LEONARD LLC
International Copyright Secured   All Rights Reserved

ONCE TO EVERY MAN AND NATION

Inspired by Beethoven's Symphony No. 7

Words by JAMES RUSSELL LOWELL
Music by THOMAS J. WILLIAMS
Arranged by Phillip Keveren

Solemnly (♩ = 60)

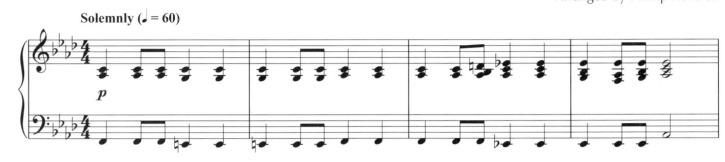

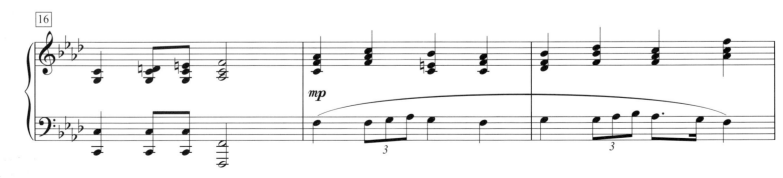

Copyright © 2017 by HAL LEONARD LLC
International Copyright Secured   All Rights Reserved

PRAISE TO THE LORD, THE ALMIGHTY

Words by JOACHIM NEANDER
Translated by CATHERINE WINKWORTH
Music from *Erneuerten Gesangbuch*
Arranged by Phillip Keveren

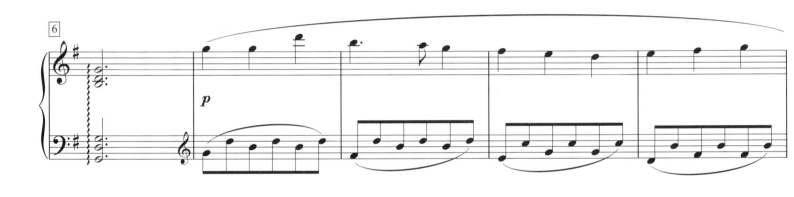

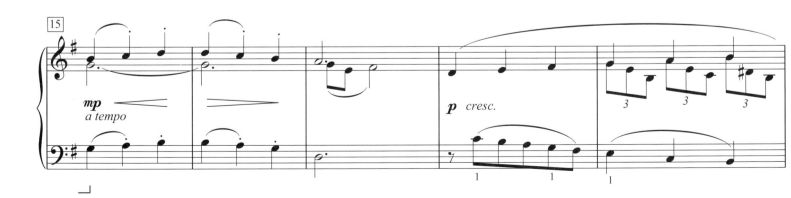

Copyright © 2003 by HAL LEONARD CORPORATION
International Copyright Secured   All Rights Reserved

ROCK OF AGES

Music by THOMAS HASTINGS
Arranged by Phillip Keveren

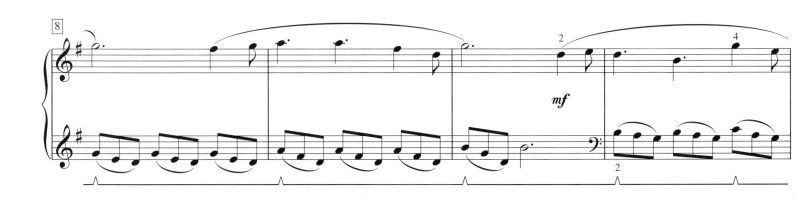

Copyright © 2018 by HAL LEONARD LLC
International Copyright Secured   All Rights Reserved

SPIRIT OF GOD, DESCEND UPON MY HEART

Words by GEORGE CROLY
Music by FREDERICK COOK ATKINSON
Arranged by Phillip Keveren

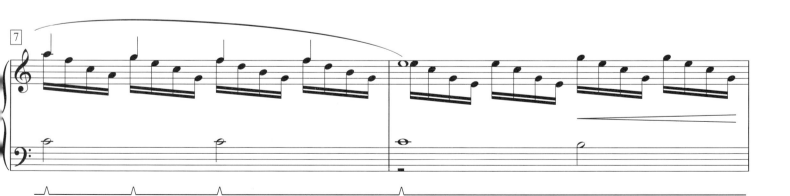

Copyright © 2011 by HAL LEONARD CORPORATION
International Copyright Secured   All Rights Reserved

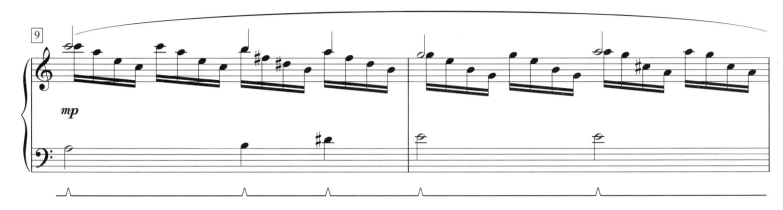

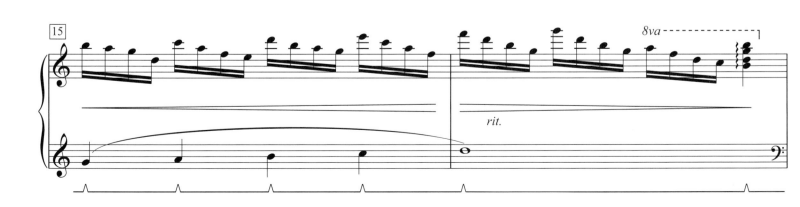

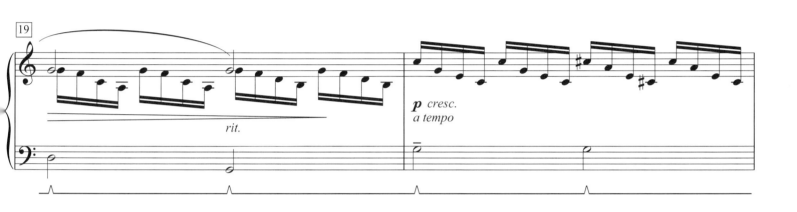

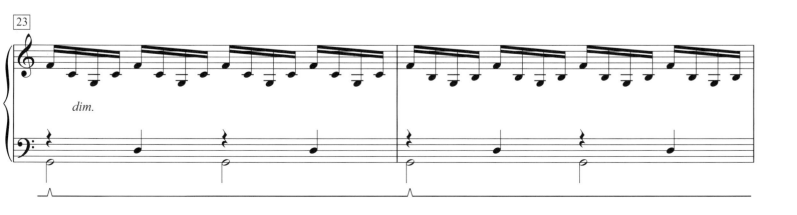

SAVIOR, LIKE A SHEPHERD LEAD US

Words from *Hymns For The Young*
Attributed to DOROTHY A. THRUPP
Music by WILLIAM B. BRADBURY
Arranged by Phillip Keveren

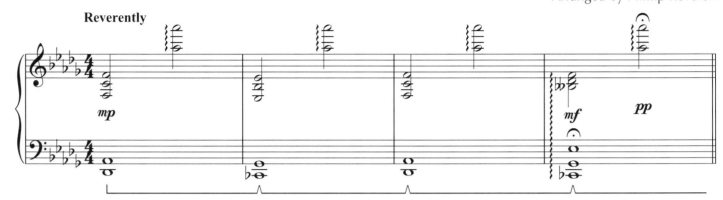

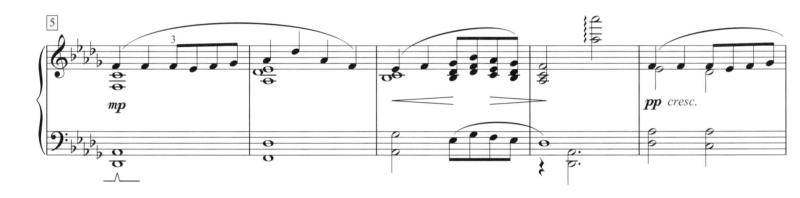

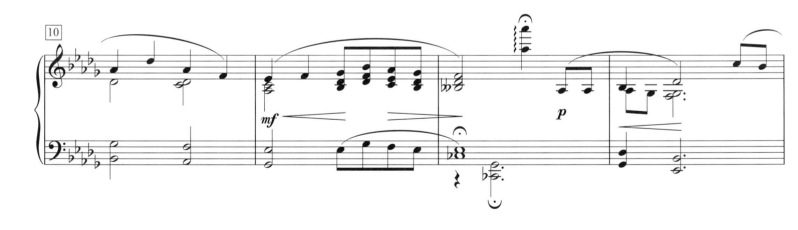

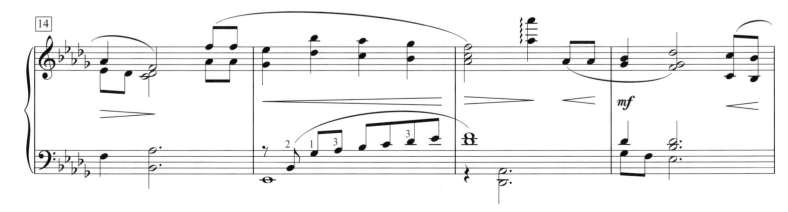

Copyright © 2005 by HAL LEONARD CORPORATION
International Copyright Secured   All Rights Reserved

THERE IS A BALM IN GILEAD

African American Spiritual
Arranged by Phillip Keveren

Copyright © 2010 by HAL LEONARD CORPORATION
International Copyright Secured   All Rights Reserved

THIS IS MY FATHER'S WORLD

Words by MALTBIE D. BABCOCK
Music by FRANKLIN L. SHEPPARD
Arranged by Phillip Keveren

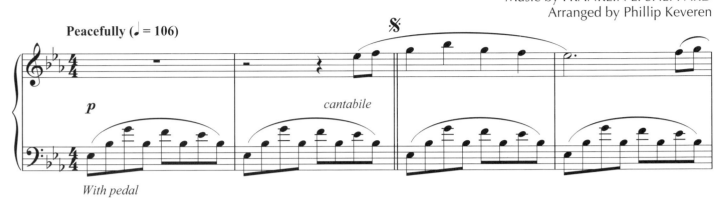

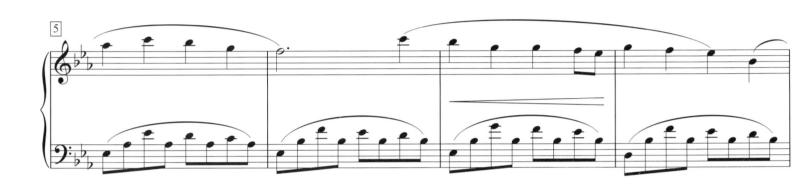

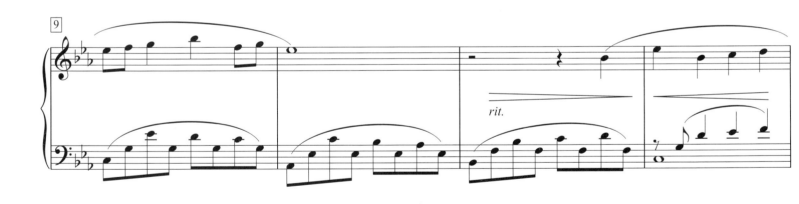

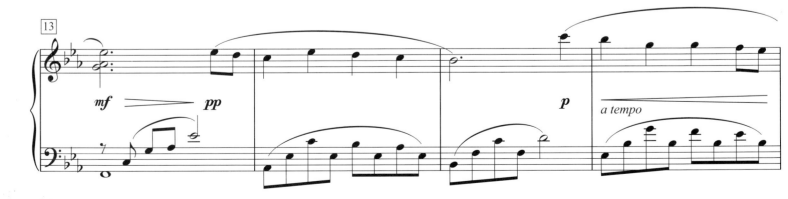

Copyright © 2003 by HAL LEONARD CORPORATION
International Copyright Secured   All Rights Reserved

WE ARE CLIMBING JACOB'S LADDER

African American Spiritual
Arranged by Phillip Keveren

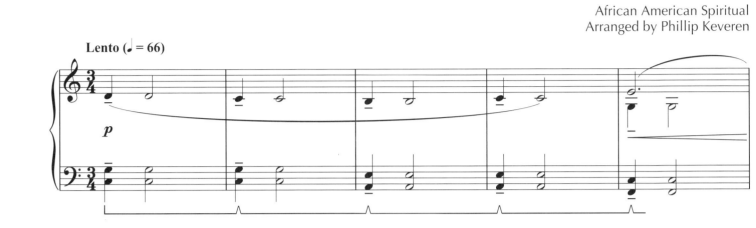

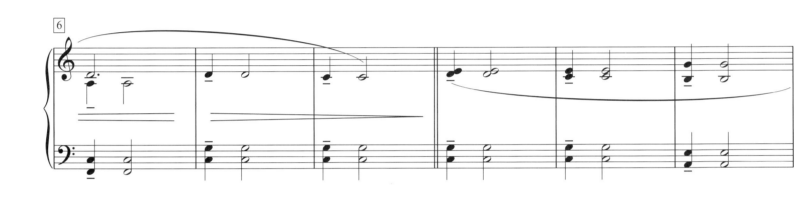

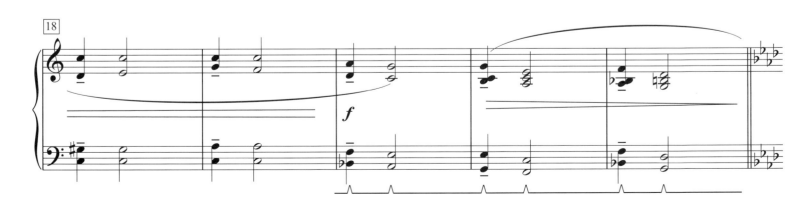

Copyright © 2006 by HAL LEONARD CORPORATION
International Copyright Secured   All Rights Reserved

WE GATHER TOGETHER

Netherlands Folk Hymn
Translated by THEODORE BAKER
Music from *Nederlandtsch Gedenckclanck*
Harmonized by EDUARD KREMSER
Arranged by Phillip Keveren

Copyright © 2021 by HAL LEONARD LLC
International Copyright Secured   All Rights Reserved

WERE YOU THERE?

Traditional Spiritual
Arranged by Phillip Keveren

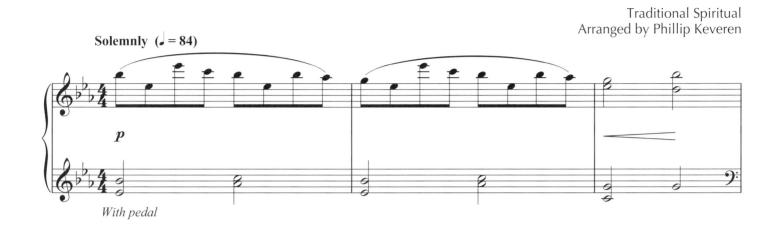

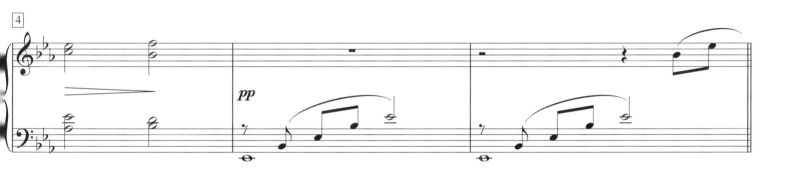

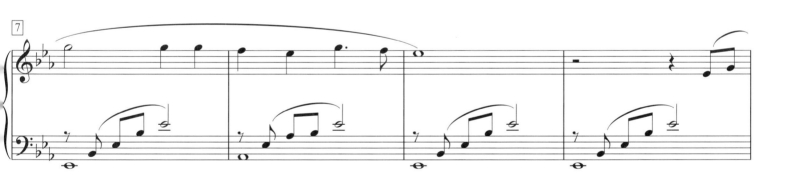

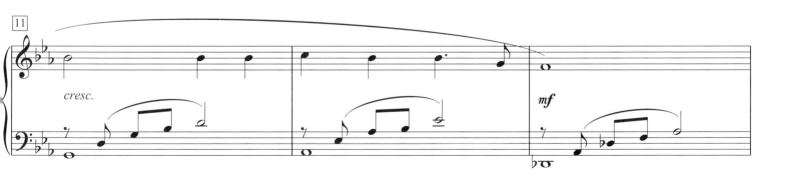

Copyright © 2003 by HAL LEONARD CORPORATION
International Copyright Secured   All Rights Reserved

142

WHAT A FRIEND WE HAVE IN JESUS

Words by JOSEPH M. SCRIVEN
Music by CHARLES C. CONVERSE
Arranged by Phillip Keveren

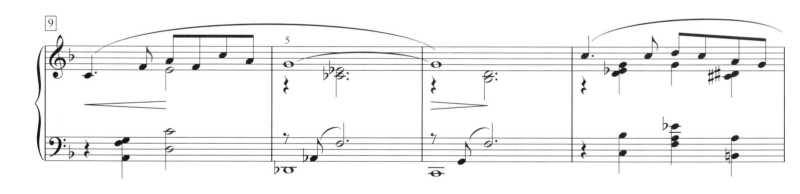

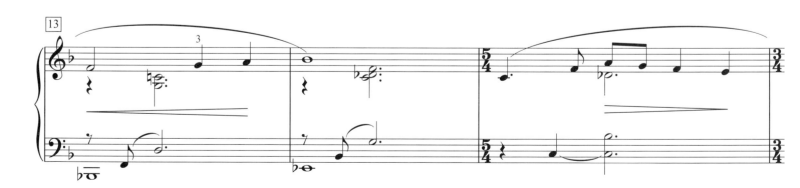

Copyright © 2005 by HAL LEONARD CORPORATION
International Copyright Secured   All Rights Reserved

APPENDIX

*The hymns in bold are featured in **The Essential Hymn Anthology.**

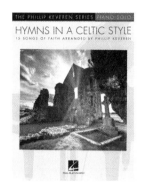

280705   HYMNS IN A CELTIC STYLE

All Creatures of Our God and King • Be Thou My Vision • Come, Ye Thankful People, Come • For the Beauty of the Earth • God Will Take Care of You • How Firm a Foundation • **I Sing the Mighty Power of God** • Immortal, Invisible • **The Lord's My Shepherd, I'll Not Want** • **Morning Has Broken** • **O Worship the King** • Praise God, from Whom All Blessings Flow • Praise to the Lord, the Almighty • Savior, Like a Shepherd Lead Us • What Wondrous Love Is This

269407   HYMNS WITH A CLASSICAL FLAIR

Amazing Grace • Blessed Assurance • Fairest Lord Jesus • **Faith of Our Fathers** • **His Eye is on the Sparrow** • How Firm a Foundation • **In the Garden** • Just A Closer Walk With Thee • Nearer, My God, to Thee • The Old Rugged Cross • **Rock of Ages** • Softly and Tenderly • Take My Life and Let It Be • Were You There? • What a Friend We Have in Jesus

311071   THE HYMN COLLECTION

All Hail the Power of Jesus' Name • Breathe on Me, Breath of God • **Come, Thou Almighty King** • Come, Thou Fount of Every Blessing • **Crown Him with Many Crowns** • God the Omnipotent! • God Will Take Care of You • I Love to Tell the Story • **I Surrender All** • I've Got Peace Like a River • Immortal, Invisible • O Worship the King • **Praise to the Lord, the Almighty** • Softly and Tenderly • **This Is My Father's World** • Tis So Sweet to Trust in Jesus • Were You There?

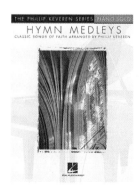

311349 HYMN MEDLEYS

Abide with Me • All Creatures of Our God and King • All Hail the Power of Jesus' Name • Bright and Beautiful • Come, Thou Fount of Every Blessing • Fairest Lord Jesus • Have Thine Own Way, Lord • **Holy, Holy, Holy! Lord God Almighty** • I Sing the Mighty Power of God • I Surrender All • **I've Got Peace Like a River** • **Immortal, Invisible** • **It Is Well with My Soul** • Joyful, Joyful, We Adore Thee • The Lord's My Shepherd, I'll Not Want • **A Mighty Fortress Is Our God** • **Nothing But the Blood** • **The Old Rugged Cross** • Praise The Lord! Ye Heavens, Adore Him • Praise to the Lord, The Almighty • This Is My Father's World • What a Friend We Have in Jesus • **When I Survey the Wondrous Cross** • **Wonderful Peace**

311249 HYMNS WITH A TOUCH OF JAZZ

Come, Thou Fount of Every Blessing • Come, Thou Long-Expected Jesus • **Fairest Lord Jesus** • God Will Take Care Of You • **I Love to Tell The Story** • I've Got Peace Like a River • **Jesus Is All the World to Me** • Jesus, the Very Thought of Thee • Just a Closer Walk with Thee • Praise to the Lord, The Almighty • **Savior, Like a Shepherd Lead Us** • Softly and Tenderly • Stand Up, Stand Up for Jesus • This Is My Father's World • **What a Friend We Have in Jesus**

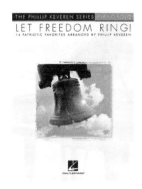

310839 LET FREEDOM RING

America, the Beautiful • Anchors Aweigh • **Battle Hymn of the Republic** • **Eternal Father, Strong to Save** • God Bless Our Native Land • God of Our Fathers • **My Country, 'Tis of Thee (America)** • Semper Fidelis • The Star-Spangled Banner • Stars and Stripes Forever • Washington Post March • Yankee Doodle • Yankee Doodle Boy • You're a Grand Old Flag

311978 THE SPIRITUALS COLLECTION

All My Trials • **Deep River** • Every Time I Feel the Spirit • He's Got the Whole World In His Hands • **We Are Climbing Jacob's Ladder** • Joshua (Fit the Battle of Jericho) • **Let Us Break Bread Together** • The Lonesome Road • Somebody's Knockin' At Your Door • Sometimes I Feel Like a Motherless Child • Steal Away (Steal Away to Jesus) • Swing Low, Sweet Chariot • **There Is a Balm In Gilead** • Wayfaring Stranger • **Were You There?**

224738 SYMPHONIC HYMNS FOR PIANO

All Creatures of Our God and King • **At Calvary** • Bright and Beautiful • **Christ the Lord Is Risen Today** • The Church's One Foundation • For the Beauty of the Earth • God So Loved the World • **He Hideth My Soul** • His Eye Is On the Sparrow • **I Need Thee Every Hour** • Jesus Loves Even Me (I Am So Glad) • Living for Jesus • Now Thank We All Our God • **Once to Every Man and Nation** • Rejoice, the Lord Is King • Tell Me the Stories of Jesus • We've a Story to Tell to the Nations

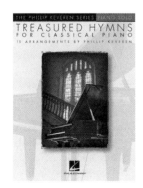

312112 TREASURED HYMNS FOR CLASSICAL PIANO

Abide with Me • All Creatures of Our God and King • **Be Thou My Vision** • For the Beauty of the Earth • **Guide Me, O Thou Great Jehovah** • Holy, Holy, Holy! Lord God Almighty • I Sing the Mighty Power of God • The Lord's My Shepherd, I'll Not Want • A Mighty Fortress Is Our God • **O Love That Wilt Not Let Me Go** • O Worship the King • Praise God, From Whom All Blessings Flow • Praise to the Lord, The Almighty • **Spirit of God, Descend Upon My Heart** • We Gather Together

THE PHILLIP KEVEREN SERIES

PIANO SOLO

00156644	**ABBA for Classical Piano**	$15.99
00311024	**Above All**	$12.99
00311348	**Americana**	$12.99
00198473	**Bach Meets Jazz**	$14.99
00313594	**Bacharach and David**	$15.99
00306412	**The Beatles**	$19.99
00312189	**The Beatles for Classical Piano**	$17.99
00275876	**The Beatles – Recital Suites**	$19.99
00312546	**Best Piano Solos**	$15.99
00156601	**Blessings**	$14.99
00198656	**Blues Classics**	$14.99
00284359	**Broadway Songs with a Classical Flair**	$14.99
00310669	**Broadway's Best**	$16.99
00312106	**Canzone Italiana**	$12.99
00280848	**Carpenters**	$17.99
00310629	**A Celtic Christmas**	$14.99
00310549	**The Celtic Collection**	$14.99
00280571	**Celtic Songs with a Classical Flair**	$12.99
00263362	**Charlie Brown Favorites**	$14.99
00312190	**Christmas at the Movies**	$15.99
00294754	**Christmas Carols with a Classical Flair**	$12.99
00311414	**Christmas Medleys**	$14.99
00236669	**Christmas Praise Hymns**	$12.99
00233788	**Christmas Songs for Classical Piano**	$14.99
00311769	**Christmas Worship Medleys**	$14.99
00310607	**Cinema Classics**	$15.99
00301857	**Circles**	$10.99
00311101	**Classic Wedding Songs**	$12.99
00311292	**Classical Folk**	$10.95
00311083	**Classical Jazz**	$14.99
00137779	**Coldplay for Classical Piano**	$16.99
00311103	**Contemporary Wedding Songs**	$12.99
00348788	**Country Songs with a Classical Flair**	$14.99
00249097	**Disney Recital Suites**	$17.99
00311754	**Disney Songs for Classical Piano**	$17.99
00241379	**Disney Songs for Ragtime Piano**	$17.99
00364812	**The Essential Hymn Anthology**	$34.99
00311881	**Favorite Wedding Songs**	$14.99
00315974	**Fiddlin' at the Piano**	$12.99
00311811	**The Film Score Collection**	$15.99
00269408	**Folksongs with a Classical Flair**	$12.99
00144353	**The Gershwin Collection**	$14.99
00233789	**Golden Scores**	$14.99
00144351	**Gospel Greats**	$14.99
00183566	**The Great American Songbook**	$14.99
00312084	**The Great Melodies**	$14.99
00311157	**Great Standards**	$14.99
00171621	**A Grown-Up Christmas List**	$14.99
00311071	**The Hymn Collection**	$14.99
00311349	**Hymn Medleys**	$14.99
00280705	**Hymns in a Celtic Style**	$14.99

00269407	**Hymns with a Classical Flair**	$14.99
00311249	**Hymns with a Touch of Jazz**	$14.99
00310905	**I Could Sing of Your Love Forever**	$16.99
00310762	**Jingle Jazz**	$15.99
00175310	**Billy Joel for Classical Piano**	$16.99
00126449	**Elton John for Classical Piano**	$19.99
00310839	**Let Freedom Ring!**	$12.99
00238988	**Andrew Lloyd Webber Piano Songbook**	$14.99
00313227	**Andrew Lloyd Webber Solos**	$17.99
00313523	**Mancini Magic**	$16.99
00312113	**More Disney Songs for Classical Piano**	$16.99
00311295	**Motown Hits**	$14.99
00300640	**Piano Calm**	$12.99
00339131	**Piano Calm: Christmas**	$14.99
00346009	**Piano Calm: Prayer**	$14.99
00306870	**Piazzolla Tangos**	$17.99
00386709	**Praise and Worship for Classical Piano**	$14.99
00156645	**Queen for Classical Piano**	$17.99
00310755	**Richard Rodgers Classics**	$17.99
00289545	**Scottish Songs**	$12.99
00119403	**The Sound of Music**	$16.99
00311978	**The Spirituals Collection**	$12.99
00366023	**So Far…**	$14.99
00210445	**Star Wars**	$16.99
00224738	**Symphonic Hymns for Piano**	$14.99
00366022	**Three-Minute Encores**	$16.99
00279673	**Tin Pan Alley**	$12.99
00312112	**Treasured Hymns for Classical Piano**	$15.99
00144926	**The Twelve Keys of Christmas**	$14.99
00278486	**The Who for Classical Piano**	$16.99
00294036	**Worship with a Touch of Jazz**	$14.99
00311911	**Yuletide Jazz**	$19.99

EASY PIANO

00210401	**Adele for Easy Classical Piano**	$17.99
00310610	**African-American Spirituals**	$12.99
00218244	**The Beatles for Easy Classical Piano**	$14.99
00218387	**Catchy Songs for Piano**	$12.99
00310973	**Celtic Dreams**	$12.99
00233686	**Christmas Carols for Easy Classical Piano**	$14.99
00311126	**Christmas Pops**	$16.99
00368199	**Christmas Reflections**	$14.99
00311548	**Classic Pop/Rock Hits**	$14.99
00310769	**A Classical Christmas**	$14.99
00310975	**Classical Movie Themes**	$12.99
00144352	**Disney Songs for Easy Classical Piano**	$14.99
00311093	**Early Rock 'n' Roll**	$14.99
00311997	**Easy Worship Medleys**	$14.99
00289547	**Duke Ellington**	$14.99
00160297	**Folksongs for Easy Classical Piano**	$12.99

00110374	**George Gershwin Classics**	$14.99
00310805	**Gospel Treasures**	$14.99
00306821	**Vince Guaraldi Collection**	$19.99
00160294	**Hymns for Easy Classical Piano**	$14.99
00310798	**Immortal Hymns**	$12.99
00311294	**Jazz Standards**	$12.99
00355474	**Living Hope**	$14.99
00310744	**Love Songs**	$14.99
00233740	**The Most Beautiful Songs for Easy Classical Piano**	$12.99
00220036	**Pop Ballads**	$14.99
00311406	**Pop Gems of the 1950s**	$12.95
00233739	**Pop Standards for Easy Classical Piano**	$12.99
00102887	**A Ragtime Christmas**	$12.99
00311293	**Ragtime Classics**	$14.99
00312028	**Santa Swings**	$14.99
00233688	**Songs from Childhood for Easy Classical Piano**	$12.99
00103258	**Songs of Inspiration**	$14.99
00310840	**Sweet Land of Liberty**	$12.99
00126450	**10,000 Reasons**	$16.99
00310712	**Timeless Praise**	$14.99
00311086	**TV Themes**	$14.99
00310717	**21 Great Classics**	$14.99
00160076	**Waltzes & Polkas for Easy Classical Piano**	$12.99
00145342	**Weekly Worship**	$17.99

BIG-NOTE PIANO

00310838	**Children's Favorite Movie Songs**	$14.99
00346000	**Christmas Movie Magic**	$12.99
00277368	**Classical Favorites**	$12.99
00277370	**Disney Favorites**	$14.99
00310888	**Joy to the World**	$12.99
00310908	**The Nutcracker**	$12.99
00277371	**Star Wars**	$16.99

BEGINNING PIANO SOLOS

00311202	**Awesome God**	$14.99
00310837	**Christian Children's Favorites**	$14.99
00311117	**Christmas Traditions**	$10.99
00311250	**Easy Hymns**	$12.99
00102710	**Everlasting God**	$10.99
00311403	**Jazzy Tunes**	$10.95
00310822	**Kids' Favorites**	$12.99
00367778	**A Magical Christmas**	$14.99
00338175	**Silly Songs for Kids**	$9.99

PIANO DUET

00126452	**The Christmas Variations**	$14.99
00362562	**Classic Piano Duets**	$14.99
00311350	**Classical Theme Duets**	$12.99
00295099	**Gospel Duets**	$12.99
00311544	**Hymn Duets**	$14.99
00311203	**Praise & Worship Duets**	$14.99
00294755	**Sacred Christmas Duets**	$14.99
00119405	**Star Wars**	$16.99
00253545	**Worship Songs for Two**	$12.99

HAL•LEONARD®

Search songlists, more products and place your order from your favorite music retailer at **halleonard.com**

Disney characters and artwork
TM & © 2021 Disney LLC

Prices, contents, and availability subject to change without notice.

0422
158